Living Moments

Living Moments

A Collection of Creative Works

Warren Sunkar

Copyright © 2020 Warren Sunkar

The moral right of the author has been asserted.

All rights reserved.
No part of this publication may be reproduced, stored in a retrieval system, or transmitted, in any form or by any means, without the prior permission in writing of the publisher, nor be otherwise circulated in any form of binding or cover other than that in which it is published and without a similar condition including this condition being imposed on the subsequent purchaser.

 A catalogue record for this book is available from the National Library of Australia

Creator: Sunkar, Warren, author.

Title: Living Moments / Warren Sunkar.

ISBN: 978-0-9953716-4-4 (paperback)

Layout: Pickawoowoo Publishing Group (Interior and cover)

Table of Contents

Great Mother of the Stars · 1
In Chorus with Wolves · 2
Child of Light · 5
Ayahuasca Dreaming · 13
Gaia Laments · 22
The Oracle · 25
Thinking In A Thoughtless World · · · · · · · · · · · · · · · · · 35
The Graveyard Vagabond · 37
Tears Upon The Battlefield · 39
So Does A Lie Meet Its End · 44
A Waltz To Remember · 49
Strange Times · 56
When The Lights Go Out… · 58
Your Reign Now Ends · 64
WOW · 68
The Left-Hand Path · 73
Through The Veil · 74
My Love · 78
Love In A Living Moment · 80

Facing Beauty · 85
A Gift From The Stars · 86
The Dawn Lovers · 90
Unutterable Love · 92
On A Starry Night · 94
Running Back Up The Mountain · · · · · · · · · · · · · · · · · · 96
Refugees Of Love · 103
What Manner Of Love Is This? · · · · · · · · · · · · · · · · · · · 105

Great Mother Of The Stars

Upon the turning of the great shift of ages,
The darkness writhes, roars, spits and rages.
Humanity trembles in confusion and fear
As we stand upon time's frontier.
Some moments awe inspiring
Other moments terrifying
Our fantastic journey has brought us here.

Oh Great Mother of the stars,
You who have come from afar,
Gently enfolding this world of death
Healing it with your sweet cosmic breath.
In these depths of such travesty
Do you reveal your Divine Majesty.
Universal Queen upon my knees do I pray
As you merge into my being, with your krystalline DNA.
Now a child of Life, Universally reborn
Called to mend the finest of fabric that has been torn.

This celestial gown of such radiant beauty.
Guide me to be more gentle,
That I may receive this grace given to me.
The honour of carrying this delicate flame
Divine rose of this heart
How I revere thee!

In Chorus With Wolves

We stood overlooking a city. In the distance, the streaming and flickering lights of neon and traffic thriving upon a circuit board of streets lit up the night sky before us through a dull smoky haze. The strange and mixed sounds of civilisation, ever constant, ever present, echoed to our ears from below. Holding one another, we looked out into the vastness of space as the Sun disappeared beyond sight and shadow spread across the world.

Babylon had risen before us...

As timid children we stand before this darkness with fluttering hearts, breathless and vulnerable as the wails of Earth reach fever pitch. Wayward humanity chained to its dying world. Hiding behind its fear and ignorance in a futile attempt to escape from that which must come to pass – do we stand today over a global civilisation that shall now collapse fast upon itself.

My friend took my hand firmly and I welcomed her.

"Has it come to this?" she whispered, as a tear ran down her cheek, her eyes reflecting my own heart's sorrow.

"What does come, must be," I whispered to her ear. "This wayward world does defy its soul and the dark night of these times settles upon us. This world's lost children in their defiance and arrogance now turn upon themselves in their futility and desperation. Humanity has denied its true birthright."

Her body shuddered as the travesty of human life opened in the great drama unfolding before us.

She wept openly. "Forgotten is the song of Love upon this Earth. A growing madness possesses the world, the darkened gods of man are failing and their keepers cry for blood. The rulers seek to throw such a chain around this world that they may break humanity's back. Loud is the cry of arrogance and falsehood; wolves circle and the shadows of fear taunt and dance around us.

"Would we dare weather this storm when it is all so hopeless?"

I answered: "Today, upon this fallen earth we walk within the growing madness and tensions of these times. Do not succumb to those waves of fear and despair that can temporarily engulf us. In these days of darkness and confusion let us find our repose in the silence of our hearts and forget not our heritage as children of God. We are called to stay true to our deepest heart's calling."

Her eyes glittered in the moonlight.

I whispered: "The veil of earth often seems so impenetrable and thick, yet these images that parade before us are not real. Do not identify with this transient reality. Though Love may seem to hide its face in such times it is ever present for those whose hearts are faithful and pure.

"These are the days warned by the prophets and seers of humanity's past. And in this darkest hour we are those who are called to stand amidst this almighty tempest.

"We are guided by the great truths sung upon the lips of those avatars who have walked this fallen earth for us. And remember, though the passing storm may eclipse the light it cannot vanquish the Sun."

Her hands tightened in mine. "I need to remember!"

"Then still yourself and surrender unto the will of the Divine Father. Let the cares of the world fall away for in truth they have no substance."

Her eyes looked deep into mine searching their depths and then together we looked up. In the timelessness of a sigh we let go as the living torch of love between us flared. The clouds of confusion and obscurity were dissolved and the light of Love divine glowed around us and a wave of ecstasy rippled and pulsed through us.

She cried out in tears of joy: "I remember!"

With the blessing of angels, in the darkest of nights, looking out over the city did we dare sing Love's song upon this fallen earth. Carried upon the winds did it find its way into the hearts of those who were open.

The earth tremored under our feet, as lightning rippled around us.

The rulers faltered, the wolves whimpered, and in their howls of fear joined us in chorus…

Our hearts gave praise.

Child Of Light

(A dream of clearing ancestral lines)

Once in the dark forest of my dreams I followed the shade of my father.

In a clouded world of mist and shadows, we journeyed through the gnarled and twisted trees, walking on the path of our ancestors, called Tradition.

We made our way with stealth and hunted with cunning. Felling many a bird from branch and sky, we left a trail of blood and scattered feathers behind us.

As we hunted, I savoured the rare words of praise my father embellished me with as each of my arrows found its mark and I could feel his look of pride upon me with each dull thud of draining life fallen upon the earth; but I could not raise my eyes to meet his stare for, in truth, I hated hunting.

Further he would beckon me into the heavy mists and shadows; foolishly I followed. I dared not question him or his intentions lest his eyes of pride look upon me no longer and he abandon me in this accursed wood. The thought of that frightened me; for often, to myself, I wondered if he knew where we were going at all, for as I looked down to my feet to question the path that we were walking, I became fearful and confused because there didn't seem to be one.

Then, after what seemed an eternity of mindless wandering, I could go no further and I stopped. Exhausted, I massaged my aching legs and began to contemplate the senselessness of my actions. Paying no attention to the fearful calls of my father who was yelling at me about the dangers of staying still, I broke down in tears at the pointlessness of it all.

Then, sung out of the darkness, carried upon the dank heavy airs that swirled about us sounded a low and sorrowful moaning. Frozen in my fear, I listened attentively as does a terrified rabbit that listens for the sound of a nearby fox, absolutely still and with a pounding heart. The dreadful cries grew deeper, seeming to reverberate from the very depths of my dark little world, sung with such anguish and hopelessness like a mournful spectre who waits for the light of heavenly acceptance that doesn't come.

Retaining but only a few drops of my evaporated courage, I silently crept through the dense undergrowth towards such misery's source.

From behind a bush I inhaled deeply as I drew back its branches...

Piercing through the dark clouds of my inner world, the forgotten Sun shone a ray of Love to illuminate a small forest clearing. In the centre of the clearing kneeled a lone, sadly man. He was a monk. His robes were but rags, they were tattered and torn. His face sullen, his features partially hidden behind a long and thick matted beard on which hung a fine webbing of thin icicles spun by the spinnerets of the ice spider, Frost. His hair, knotted and wild, was tossed back as his tear-filled eyes beseeched the skies for forgiveness. Within his cupped and blood-washed hands he held the crumpled form of a dead white dove which he raised in offering to the heavens.

Held fast, I stared at the scene before me in confusion and fear raced down my spine like the cold hand of a ghost passing through me as I realised the dead dove he held within his hands was one of the birds I had felled.

His cry came to a sudden stop and my heart skipped a beat for I knew he had sensed our presence. Turning around, he stared directly into my eyes with a gaze so powerful I felt as if the hand of God was around me, able to crush my bones to powder if he so willed it. Rising to his feet, he walked to the edge of the light with the dead, limp dove loosely held within his fingers.

Hypnotised, I was fixed as stone and time was suspended. Then, from the shadows, my father stepped out to protect me, his hunting bow ready and aimed. Breaking the gaze that held me fast, I exhaled sharply for I had forgotten to breathe.

"Step into the light child," spoke the monk. His tone soft, his voice was like a gentle song whispered from many different directions and was in great contrast to his deep, powerful eyes that felt like they had stripped me to my essence. Undisturbed by the shade's threatening presence, he ignored my father and kept his eyes stayed on me.

"Step into the light child," he said again.

The spirits of uncertainty had stolen my will. Mesmerised, I knew not what to say or do. Sensing my hesitation, his face grew softer and his tone outreaching as he gestured out into the shadows: "Step into the light child for there are worse things than I out there."

"What do you want?" I managed to stammer, my voice scared and deflated.

"Fear me not." His voice was soothing and calm. "I have come for you."

Confused, I timidly asked, "Why are you here?"

Keeping me stilled within his gaze he spoke "For I have wandered through this wood of human misconception for thousands of years, finding the lost and healing the brokenhearted. For thousands of years I have nurtured life within these realms only to have you take it away. This woeful era of senselessness is at its end and now humanity will learn responsibility for itself. It is time to reveal to you a new path; it is time for the children of Earth to walk the true way; it is time to lay down your bow and hunt no longer."

He continued: "I am here because tradition has become but a path of ignorance and your way has lost its meaning. I am here because in your dreams you are crying for truth. The complacency of aimlessness you have indulged in has become restrictive torture. I am here to tell you to release your grip upon your suffering for it is by your own hand that you strangle yourself. Step into the light child for out there in the shadows there is only slavery. Out there in the darkness of egoism all is illusion."

Struggling with his words I flared up with frustration. "You would have me lay down my bow and leave me helpless in this savage wood? I say it is you who has lost your way," I spat back. His words had burned me.

A gentle smile warmed his face. "Aye, I would have you lay down your bow but you will not be helpless. Verily, I will help make you a giant if you but embrace the truth of who you are. Only in gentleness and compassion can humanity grow, and a giant you will become when you realise that the greatest powers lie latent in the depths of humility.

"For in vulnerability you will find the greatest strength.

"And understand you will that the finest armour is openness and only in obedience will you find true freedom."

"You speak to me in riddles," I shot back, confused.

"Nay, it is your life that has fallen into a riddle," he replied. "I offer its solution. Here in the ray of heavenly Love, the shades of perception disappear within the light of Truth. Here all darkness is vanquished."

Silenced, I tried to absorb all that he was saying.

His face dropped in sadness as his eyes swelled with tears. Holding the dead bird forward, cupped in his bloodied hands, he softly spoke: "She is of you, yet you know it not."

Confused, I stammered, "She is just a bird."

And he answered sadly: "Child of Earth, would you stay blind? If this is just a bird, then this is but a dream and I will bid you farewell for it is your choice to remain in the darkness."

Despair welled within me and panicking, I pleaded: "Please don't leave me."

Gesturing the bird towards me he whispered: "She is of you child and she is more than just a bird, understand that; she is the delicate flame of inspiration blown out by the breath of ignorance; she is love pierced by a dart of thoughtlessness; she is an unanswered prayer, fallen back into the void."

Tears streamed down his face as he explained softly: "With each life that you claim, you kill part of yourself. With each step further into darkness you take, the colder you become." Pleading, he reached out his hand and asked: "Lay down your bow child, take my hand; it is time to end this foolishness."

I went to walk to him but my father hissed, his bow raised in protection, keeping me behind him.

The monk turned toward the shade and with authority spoke: "Be gone illusion of yesterday, you will lead no more. Be gone minion of fear, you are but a shadow of what is because your way is lost in what has been. The children of Earth will be deluded no longer."

As the monk continued, the shade began to tremble. "Let you not make your child stand behind you, but you behind your child for it is through children that Life expresses itself. Life is eternal progression and renewal, it cannot be stayed. So I say unto you that he who tries to stay Life with the hand of ignorance will be thwarted by himself, for he acts contrary to his own true nature; and he who holds back the children of Life is fear of Life itself. Be gone!"

Then, with a firm gaze and gesture he dismissed my father. Powerless, the shade lowered his bow and resigned subserviently, stepping back into the shadows behind me.

LIVING MOMENTS

Turning back to face me, the monk's eyes looked at me deeply. "In truth, all fathers are but children following in the footsteps of their own. Had you true sight you would have seen your father as a child, being beckoned onwards by his own fear and then realised the disastrous plight of humanity, that it is lost and walking in circles. Such is the foolishness of man. I have seen sons bury their fathers to be buried by their sons in a grim procession of eternal death. It is to be no longer, the cycle of ignorance ends with you.

"Step into the light child, it is Love. Lay down your bow and embrace me for I am eternal Life."

Drawing upon my courage, I laid down my bow and, taking a step forward, I accepted his hand. Leaving the darkness of my lower nature, I stepped into the light. Behind me I could hear the shade crying out in desperation and fear — it was repentant and frightened but I did not look back. I was beyond its grasp and I knew all was to be forgiven.

Absorbed into the light I was met in Love as I embraced my divine self and, in a flash of union, we became One. There in the light of Truth, all darkness was vanquished and the flame of ecstasy raced through me as tears of joy streamed down my face. Raising the dead white dove I held within my fingers, I brought it to my lips. There in the light of understanding, I gently kissed it with the breath of Life and released it into the air...

That day, in the forest of my dreams, a lone white dove spiralled into the sky higher than any arrow could reach her. Her cries of freedom and love echoed throughout my world, causing all the trees to yield up their birds into the sky. Leading them up into the heavens, she pierced through the dark clouds of obscurity that had always been there and the divine sun broke through in brilliant colour and unutterable revelation. I fell to my knees in tearful bliss; never would I be lost again.

I had found Love divine.

Then I woke up…

(Written at age twenty-two)

Ayahuasca Dreaming

It was just after sunset and we sat upon the floor.

As I poured the brown liquid I briefly pondered the unexpected synchronicities that had brought us together for such an event. A tingling sensation went through my body and I was aware that the plant was speaking to me. I smiled. We had heard the stories of others and now it was time for an experience of our own.

It was said that the Teacher Plant had a consciousness that would communicate with those who received it with an open mind and heart.

In an unspoken trust we shared a couple of bowls of the brew between us not knowing what to expect and the four of us downed the bitter potion with distaste.

As the bowls were drained, we lay upon our backs surrendering to a metaphysical journey into the unknown…

Staring at the ceiling, slow conscious minutes ticked by.

Nestling into the thin mattress underneath me, my sense of self began to gently dissipate into a soft ethereal glow that infused me with splashes of warmth that washed through my body.

Rising, dissolving, expanding into greater freedom, my diminishing consciousness of time slowly began dissolving in vapours of love as my awareness of five-sense reality began melting like butter upon a stovetop.

Relaxing, we lightened to become unexpectedly aware of a spritely spirit of Earth. Feminine and playful, she darted and hovered between us in a loving and flirtatious dance. Playing with us in a sensual and unabashed manner she caressed all those who were in the room. Diving through the air, she washed herself through me, kissing me on my lips as I laughed in delighted surprise.

I could feel her healing ethereal touches all over my body as her voice whispered beautiful imagery into my mind as my body shivered in blissful response.

I laughed out aloud as she poked my stomach in a soft jest to let me know she could condense and materialise.

As she played, two other kinds of earthen spirits were unveiled and lovingly nestled into my side. I lay on my back stroking them gently as they nuzzled me in a sweet affection.

As I lay there, I could hear and feel my friends around me. Each one was sharing such an experience as the spritely earth spirit swam around the room blessing each of them with her delicious aura, bathing those she touched in kisses of bliss as she whispered visions and voices of love and affirmation.

Shutting my eyes and nestling deeper into the experience, the veil of the unseen dissolved before me. We could understand that the Ayahuasca plant was a living key and energetic link to that which was the spirit of the earth.

Suddenly, I could feel the ethers above us deeply stir as a dimensional portal opened.

A quickening pulse took me from within and I felt the presence of the Great Guardian.

I looked up as this ultra-terrestrial of light opened the gateway above me to touch my aura with its rainbow of colours and energies.

Unlocking within a deep remembrance, I felt a strong kinship and affiliation with this great multi-dimensional intelligence and I gasped in splendour as this benevolent insectoid drew back the dimensional veils between us and the vibrations of light quickened through the room to engulf us all.

Shutting my eyes, I was raised into an exploding fractal vision of shimmering colours and cascading rivers of pulsing living energies. Waves of ecstasy washed through my body as I launched into the pool of lights around me.

A chameleon of changing vibrations, I shifted gently yet swiftly through the thin veils of dimension – twirling and spinning in a dance of joy with the ease and grace enlivened from a remembrance, and experienced beyond the confines of body consciousness.

Suddenly, I found myself standing in a jungle clearing.

Bright psychic light shimmered all around as exotic birds and insects in symphony adorned the spectacular vision of the world I stood in.

Before me stood four shamans. They were ancient ones, powerful and impressive as they bowed solemnly. Awe inspiring in their headdress of colourful plumage, I bowed in the presence of these teachers. Then in silence we sat in a circle and communed with closed eyes.

I began to fall backwards and upwards into the vast expanse of space as images flashed rapidly through my mind's eye in a collage of information.

I received a forgotten history of secret and dark things. All hidden today behind a movie version of reality, within which we are manipulated and maintained by the nefarious keepers of our world. I cried out in horror as alien beings looked upon humanity with cold, predatory eyes.

A profound sadness took my heart as before me opened a storyboard of tragedy. Holding me in an embrace of love, the Teacher Plant guided me to a deeper understanding of the mostly unseen happenings here upon Earth.

Humanity's sad history entwined with these Greys.

These lost and foreign beings had altered the human race by genetically tampering, implanting and controlling them. Humanity has been not unlike lab rats to these foreign beings and I reeled before the sickening vision of what has happened in humanity's past and what goes on still today from the shadows.

The visions and teachings came with an increasing rapidity which downloaded through my awareness as the Teacher Plant communicated, helping me to understand and remember. I opened further into the experience, trusting the guidance to see the truth of the planetary situation.

The anguish of humanity took my heart as I was expanded to see how humanity was being kept from its true potentiality.

How we are all being manipulated into a vibratory prison with most of the populace unknowing of their fate.

Upon this Earth, all are subject to occult enslavement and are energetically paralysed by those beings that exist outside the now extremely limited bandwidth of humanity's vibratory perception.

I shuddered as I saw within the dark subterranean levels of the planet reptilians hissing from the shadows.

Falling backwards I became aware once again of the presence of my friends.

The greater light pervading the room and us all from within, dissolved any sense of separation as we had all melded as one in psychic unity.

We were as open books to one another, and nothing was kept hidden as we accessed each other's thought streams and life waves. Hidden secrets, joys and fears were shared between us as visual transmissions as the night went on slipping in and out of a timeless blur.

As each of our lives unravelled before one another, they were played out almost cinematically. It enabled us to observe each other's burdens, weaknesses and lives without judgement or condemnation as we all saw from the greater perspective.

We rejoiced in the experience for there were only smiles in such a union as the Teacher Plant guided us all through the moment with a loving embrace.

I became aware of my partner lying upon a couch behind me, beginning to stir as the Teacher Plant revealed to her that which she found difficult to accept.

Following her energy stream, I opened to her, sharing a vision of great tribulations coming to the planet. She witnessed humanity losing itself to madness and savagery, opening itself to planetary destruction.

She was openly weeping and shaking her head at such a possibility. I was inwardly motioned to go to her. I knelt next to the couch and gently put my arms around her as she burrowed into my chest. Holding her, comforting her, I ran my hands through her hair as she curled foetally, tears running down her cheeks.

As I shut my eyes again a pre-Earth remembrance awoke from within both of us.

As stars we flew through space beyond the heavy and suffocating clouds and confines of Earth's density, playing as children of Love. We saw our life threads circling and entwining in a dance of joy and innocence as we felt our connection run much deeper than the short relationship that we share in our earthly personalities.

Then we saw others of our greater family, stars of light, responding to the cry of Gaia and her humanity as we answered in a wave of Love to descend and penetrate into the darkened sphere of Earth, to seed this planet for its birth into its cosmic initiation.

The night sped on as we all throbbed in ecstasy, plunged into a vortex of imagery and unutterable revelation, unfiltered by the limitations of mind.

Each message personal yet shared, with each of us taking that which was meant for them. The playful spirit darted and danced between us all, giving healings and comfort as each of us gasped or laughed at the revelations and messages given them.

Then softly, in an inner dawning of soul stirring and arousing, not unlike a soft crescendo of a playing violin, a haunting song arose within the inner silence and its deep sadness began to take my heart as everything faded into darkness.

Majestic Gaia, like a whale of the ocean depths, was singing her lament through deep space. I was flooded with the deepest of sorrow as her call brought tears streaming down my cheeks. A deep longing rose to my lips as I moaned out aloud in deepest soul pain. Humanity had forgotten their great mother and she was calling out in her great pain and distress.

As I looked out over Earth in cosmic vision from space, I knew we were failing her. Great helplessness and shame stirred from within as the acceptance of being part of the collective that was killing her washed through me.

Overwhelmed, I cried and sang back to her through the vast expanse of space.

I was sobbing.

I looked back upon a wayward humanity, out of cosmic rhythm, crippled and poisoned. I cried out to them through space but they were so immersed in themselves that they could not hear.

Humanity, if you would only open and see, you would recoil in horror and shame at the madness you have unleashed. Your loving Mother is in such pain, open your hearts to her for she is part of you and you of her. You have forgotten her sacrifice and how she has laboured for you.

She calls for her children's love and understanding.

As I was launched again through space, a portal opened, and in a surge of light and colour I was transported in a neon blur as the great cosmic womb opened before me.

Unable to resist, I merged inside.

Wave upon wave of delightful, mystical energy rippled sensually through me. I was a solar seed to fertilise and dissolve in liquid ecstasy as my whole body throbbed in deep rhythmical orgasm.

Energy pulsed through me as a cascading shower that launched through the fountainhead of my crown in unspeakable climax, sparking within and all around me a beautiful fusion in a glorious explosion of light; a conception took place.

Crowned in mystical euphoria, a bright rainbow of light shone through me as the Guardian further opened my awareness.

With spurts of energy that flooded through me, I was encoded with symbols of living energy like a sun shower of rain. A living language of glyphs and geometrical shapes awakening aspects of my being to things unknowable to the lower mind.

Slowly, the pulsing began to softly ease as my aura convulsed in joy and fulfilment.

I then began to feel the energy gently leave.

The Guardian and its children slowly withdrew through their dimensional vortex and the consciousness of the Teacher Plant faded from my mind's eye as the realisation of time slowly began to once again infiltrate our awareness.

LIVING MOMENTS

Our awareness of space grew as we slowly adjusted and settled back to earthly consciousness.

Laying there, glowing, I cuddled into my blanket letting go with a deep, peaceful sigh. Turning around to see smiles beaming from my friends who all just laughed aloud at the experience.

That morning, we all walked outside renewed in life as the dawning light in a halo of soft pastels christened the horizon before us. The birds in beautiful symphony made music that delighted and raised our hearts as we all greeted the coming day.

Our heightened awareness of the life glowing through us had given us a deeper communion with our Great Mother. Our vibration had been raised as such that I beheld a resonance with Gaia – unknown in this short sojourn upon this earth, now understanding her great potentiality.

With a heartfelt release I thanked the Teacher Plant as I whispered to the horizon.

And I thought…

Humanity, if you would only open your little minds and hearts to embrace your own as children of Life, you would understand. You could enjoy as do birds in their morning celebration, bathing in the light of the spiritual sun.

Gaia Laments

The flash and terrible roar
Of a great star fallen,
The anguish
Of countless worlds
And beings
Drawn into chaos
And cosmic illusion.
Behold the blue jewel
Stolen and consumed.
Raped by malefic intent,
Her children
Cast into darkness
Lost in forgetfulness,
Infiltrated and grafted
Through time and space
To cosmic misery
And terror,
And Gaia laments
The song
Of her broken heart
Ripples through the cosmos,
Her burden too heavy
As she resigns to futility
And we shudder
At the great travesty
Befallen her.

LIVING MOMENTS

In answer to her cry
We came to this world
Fracturing unity
Descending
Through vibration,
Imprinting ourselves
Upon shadow;
Threads of light
Anchored to Earth
To consummate life
Seeding the planet
In joyous union
And in answer
To her prayer.
Many have come
To witness this event
From other worlds
Spaces and densities
Places unseen
And unknown,
Quivering in hope
And anticipation
For what does come
Shall reach far beyond
This little world
And the dweller here.

And for a moment
We stand amongst you
Waiting, suffering
Wanting in expectation
Heaven does come to Earth
And the great fire
Shall descend through us
But a flash in time
And a bend in space,
Yet a memory
That shall burn
In your hearts forever
For now Gaia awakes
Opening, yearning
Unfolding to rise
Into the arms
Of her lover
And all shall share
In her blessings hereafter.

Behold the blue angel
Shining in the firmament.

The Oracle

It was mid-morning as I trekked through a lush green Australian forest.

It was a magical day. Birds and insects were in beautiful orchestra. The dew still sparkled like small diamonds from the ends of the balgas and the morning sun gently warmed my face. The rich moist aroma of the forest permeated the air as I made my way through the giant karri and jarrah trees with no real thought of a destination.

I stopped for a moment to rest against a carpet of green tree moss that blanketed a fallen timber, when a small and nimble bird darted straight past my surprised face. Landing on a tree branch only metres from where I was standing, the little red-breasted robin let out a flurry of sharp chirps, seemingly to get my attention.

I watched curiously as it took off into the air to somersault and land back on the branch before me. As I watched its display of cheerful aerobatics I felt a soft and gentle surge of uplifting energy wash through my body. Letting out another flurry of chirps the robin joyfully hopped and then darted off down a small leaf-covered track. I followed.

There was not a doubt in my mind that the bird was leading me somewhere as we made our way over logs and through the trees. The robin darted from branch to branch, where it would stop and chirp at me, never getting too far ahead and often joyfully somersaulting through the air as it went.

To my surprise the trees started to thin out quickly into the green pasture of a large overgrown paddock. As I walked over the rotting post of a fallen and corroded wire fence, I could see an old and derelict timber house. The red-breasted robin was hopping around on a branch of a karri giving an exquisite series of chirps before it darted swiftly towards the building.

As I made my way to the house I observed the remnants of an old overgrown garden. An assortment of flowers littered the area, wild, yet still flourishing around the collapsed and weathered building. It seemed to have been abandoned for decades.

The robin dashed past me once again to rest on the old rusted water tank next to the house and began to tweet very excitedly to me. Then with a final chirp it darted off to the back of the house.

I was very curious...

As I followed around the side of the building, I noticed the garden became even more untamed yet more resplendent in colour as it merged with a small wood of trees behind the house. The atmosphere had become lighter and had an ethereal quality to it, almost dreamlike and beautiful.

I looked through the assortment of colourful flowers blooming around me which revealed a tall weeping willow tree at the back of the garden. To my surprise, hanging from one of its large branches was an old rope swing and on it sat a young girl with long black hair, dressed in a gown of white and wearing a purple hooded jumper.

I looked over her as she gently swung back and forth, her face hidden by the hooded jumper. She did not make a sound.

I guessed she would have been in her late teenage years.

I stood there a little perplexed, not knowing what to think of the situation and wondering why this young female was out here, by herself, in the middle of nowhere.

Then with a chirp and the feeling of wind against my cheek, the robin darted past me once again to land on a branch just above the young girl.

The girl's swinging came to a slow stop. Her face only partially revealed as she looked up at the bird with a smile. It was tweeting very loudly and excitedly.

I started to walk up to her when her words stopped me in my tracks.

"I have been watching you Warren Sunkar."

She was looking directly ahead of herself and her face was again hidden.

I was immediately taken aback by the intent and power behind those words. I wondered how she knew my name. I was confused and just stood there wondering what to do or say next. I had no idea of who or what was talking to me.

"I have been watching you Warren Sunkar," she repeated. "You are not one of my own."

There was great power in her words but I did not feel at all threatened.

Her head turned slightly and her eyes peered through the partially opened hood as she looked at me curiously. "What are you doing here?" she asked. I felt her aura expand into mine and permeate the entire garden with a wash of her ancient but very uplifting presence.

I stayed silent, a little perplexed and in awe. Words would not come.

I knew this young girl was an oracle for whoever was really addressing me.

The atmosphere then lightened around us and I relaxed my being feeling a deep love stir in my heart. A strong wave of beautiful energy washed through me and then I knew exactly by whom I was being addressed. Before me, coming through this young girl, was the spirit of Mother Earth.

The girl then elegantly rose from the swing, her face still partially hidden under the hood she wore. I could feel and see a soft ethereal glow emanating from the girl's being, gently washing the plants and trees around her. In the bliss of her presence I could hear the flowers singing.

She took a few steps towards me. Her movement smooth and graceful as a colourful butterfly lifted from a nearby tree leaf and flew by her. I could see her smile at it with such deep love and affection that my own heart felt like it was blossoming. There was such tenderness in her gestures as she stood there marvelling like an innocent child as the butterfly danced and fluttered around her.

I felt her softly whisper to my deeper being as she enveloped me in her radiance.

We shared a silent exchange.

The energies were warm, safe and very joyful, touching my heart like a gentle kiss that raised my being to an exquisite feeling of sweetness and affection.

In response, I felt a surge of divine light come from above as an aspect of my greater being came down to anchor into my body. I spoke. "I have come from very far away to be here.

"I have come to let you know that it is time."

She stood silently before me. I felt her momentarily take in deeply what was being said.

Suddenly, I felt a slight tremor of sorrow wash through me. This time I felt a deep sadness in her voice. She asked softly, "What about my children?"

I stood there silent.

Again I felt a tremor of sorrow wash through me and her words became a little more demanding as she asked again, "What about my children?"

"It is time," I answered.

"No!" she spoke and this time I felt the tremor of a deeper pain go through my body and a rejection of my words. The atmosphere momentarily changed and went a little darker as a wave of energy washed through me that made me feel nauseous.

The young girl took another step towards me but then seemed to lurch forward in an unbalanced way. I stared at her, not really comprehending what was happening.

It was then I knew that something was not right. I could feel a deep pain within me as she stumbled. She seemed sick and as her aura darkened around her, I felt another strong wave of nausea. She staggered a step forward and she looked up at my face in deep pain. I looked into her eyes as her hood fell back around her shoulders.

What I saw next I didn't expect. My heart swelled heavily and a cry escaped from my mouth. I fell straight to my knees exhaling in my deep sadness.

She looked straight into my eyes; her face was no longer hidden. On one side of her head was a dark shadow that seemed to pulse through her body and I knew she was in great pain.

Tears openly ran down my cheeks as I saw the horrific truth and I could only watch her helplessly.

The girl's aura went dark and I felt like purging. I watched this dark unnatural frequency pulse around the side of her head; she cried out desperately in her confusion and distress.

My mind's eye played a vision of what certain alien realities were doing to her as toxic tar-like energies washed through her like poison. I saw alien machinery on Earth and from beyond contorting and crippling her, sending pulses of artificial frequencies through her body. I witnessed the devastating effects of what an ignorant humanity have been doing through their negligence and greed. It was killing her.

Helplessly on my knees I watched her writhe and my heart ached for her.

And then I heard the plea of a desperate mother, "What about my children?"

I watched her with both great admiration and sadness. Even now, with all that her humanity was doing to her, she loved them so tenderly and so deeply. She would not give up her children and I knew, if necessary, she would die for them.

I felt overwhelmed and despairing. I knew that this so-called modern civilisation mostly didn't care.

I searched my being for the words I needed. To say something that would comfort her and relieve her great pain. I did not want to fail her.

I pleaded, "I have come to remind you of your family amongst the stars and the love that awaits you there. It is time, the greater shift must come."

She rejected what I was saying. "I will not leave my children."

I held her gaze. I could sense what she was doing; she was giving her children time. I knew she was far from powerless – with one shake she could clear much of her surface and much of her pain would be gone.

Another dark pulse rippled over the side of her face and her aura went dark and again she lurched and convulsed in agony as she wailed.

For a while I stayed silent, I did not know what to do. I could see she had been stripped of so much. I cried again, I felt like a helpless idiot. This was all so surreal and dramatic but I knew the reality of what I was seeing.

No words could be written or uttered for what I was feeling. My bones ached with sadness.

In desperation words broke from my lips. "Mother, can you not feel that I love you? There are many of us who have come from so far away for this time to sing with you. We are here because we promised to come back for you because it is time you re-join us."

With effort she regained her composure and was listening to me.

I continued. "Feel this heart, you cannot stay here.

"Those of your earth children who wish to come can come if they truly want to. We who have come from the stars love and remember you. I am here to remind you of your place with us. We the children of Love are waiting for you."

She smiled softly at me and there was great sadness. I could see the remembrance and hope glinting in her eyes. In her torture, in her grief, she had almost forgotten who she really was.

As she opened to what I was saying, she seemed confused and then looked down at her body self-consciously. She then looked up at me and wept in deep shame. I could see with my inner vision her horror of the damage done to her. Our Mother Earth who was once known as the blue jewel of our solar system had been stripped and desecrated. It was nothing short of rape.

I cried again and looked into her deep ancient eyes.

But there, behind her pain, I could see her even greater determination.

In that moment, I was moved by her beauty. I would do everything I could to help her.

I whispered to her as she cried, with tears streaming down my face. "You have nothing to be ashamed of beautiful mother...especially you."

We held our gaze on each other.

I looked upon her with nothing but the deepest love and strongest admiration.

She regained her composure.

Then she walked over to where I was kneeling, and standing over me placed her hand lovingly on my cheek.

I looked up and sensed things I cannot explain. That she would endure all that she could and beyond for those she so loved. She had chosen her path and staring into her eyes I felt deeper possibilities that were hidden far from my sight. In those deep ancient eyes I felt my smallness and my blindness.

Words stumbled from my lips and I asked her as would a little child, "Open my eyes, my dear mother."

As she stood over me, I saw such a fierce resolution.

But I just wanted her pain to end.

"Soon," I whispered to her, "this will all be over and this passing age will be nothing but a fading memory. Things will be restored."

And I smiled at her and thought, what is an age but perhaps a day to one such as you.

She smiled back at me again as her hand gently trailed down my cheek. After a long moment of silence, she then turned to face the woods behind her and I watched her disappear like a fading dream into the trees.

I remember a deep tiredness washed through my body and I softly dropped, falling asleep in the warm, damp soil of the garden around me.

Hours later, I was gently aroused from my slumber by the young girl. She had no memory of the morning's events and explained to me that sometimes she would come to this place to be alone. As we talked and shared our experiences of the day, I knew we would become good friends.

As the afternoon sun slowly made its way downwards, we sat staring out over the paddock.

The oracle took my arm and rested her head on my shoulder as the small red-breasted robin sung sweetly from a nearby tree.

I shut my eyes but found little solace.

I laid a hand on the soft earth beneath me.

And I thought:

It has been hard watching you humanity, polluting and tearing up the planet with no conscience or shame. Is it so hard to take the time out from your foolish little lives to walk into nature and rest your hands upon your beautiful Earth?

Then tears began to swell as I remembered.

Just let her know that you care…

Thinking In A Thoughtless World

We sat on a bench on an urban corner. I watched in amazement as hundreds of people held up their digital cameras and mobile phones taking pictures of themselves in front of a small city monument.

My friend Jahve sat next to me browsing the day's newspaper. As he read he spoke in a concerned voice. "They are saying here that scientists are going to release thousands of satellites into space and blanket the entire Earth in Wi-Fi and other artificial signals. They are saying that an amazing new world of connection and unlimited possibility is opening to us.

"What do you think about that?" he asked.

I looked at him. "Hmmm...you ask me what I think?

"People do not understand that a devil can pose as an angel of light, or a murderer can often smile and say kind things, especially when grooming his prey. The superficial and unthinking will lead each other into the same pit, too careless to pay attention and blinded by the bright lights and neon flashing around them."

Pondering a little more on what the newspaper had stated, I then repeated, "You ask me what I think?

"That hell is but a state of psychic distortion, of realities misaligned from Life and fallen into inversion. It seems that here in Lucifer's playground people live in such deep self-absorption that they are too enthralled with themselves to care about the prison that is being built around them. Here, hell is a virtual reality game that is fun to engage and with many worlds to explore or to conquer."

It was then a young woman walked over and stood just in front of us and to our surprise began removing most of her clothing. Pulling out an iPhone on a long selfie stick she sat up on the monument and began to pose seductively, presumably, to all her online followers. Her face was covered in make-up, her cleavage pushed forward, and in a very tiny bikini she pouted and blew kisses at her camera.

We looked at her amazed. She did not seem to care about all the people gathered around and some of the cruder males whistled and encouraged her. She was playing in all the attention!

I looked back at Jahve. "You ask me what I think?

"That no one is really thinking and they have all 'outsourced their brains'. That everyone has become so inherently disconnected from Life that they and their realities are becoming ever more retarded. However, I'm certain if you would ask one of these fools the same question as they stare at their own images and reflections, I'm sure they will tell you that hell has never looked so good!"

He looked up at me from his newspaper and said, "Some of us are in big trouble aren't we?"

I just stared at him and said, "You think?"

The Graveyard Vagabond

I walk in a land of ghosts.

In a city of gravestones, I hear their cries in every word they don't speak and feel the pain in every word they do. It is a pain that burns forever within my chest because I know loneliness is an unquenchable fire. They hide in the shadows of a broken heart and cry for help but it is futile because in a world of darkness no one can find each other.

I walk in a land of ghosts.

Who whisper words of love but how can they talk of love when they draw it from an empty well?

Who use words of trust but they are disposable for they have become disposable people. They search for meaning in the meaningless and cry murder when the loving truth lets the lie kill itself because they realise that without their lies they have nothing to protect themselves with, and by destroying the truth there is nothing to remind them of who they really are.

I walk in a land of ghosts.

Empty like the land I visited before this one, for everywhere they have sucked Mother Earth's teat of all its richness and turned it into cancerous bile.

They portion it out as medicine but grow more sickly every day. Like lepers, they watch each other fall to pieces. Sweeping their digits under the carpet, they smile their toothless smiles as if nothing is wrong. Those who are born with disease only know disease…that is their legacy to their children.

Cursed with life, I walk amongst the dead, kissing the lips of corpses, trying to resuscitate those who will not be saved. I watch their restless spirits rattle their chains, and I hear their cries for salvation when I walk past. But I cast my eyes down because they can't stand that I can see right through them. They look at me strangely when I ask them to awaken because they do not know they are in a dream gone bad.

I think they hate me.

And how can I blame them?

For how can one not offend shadows when one tells them they have no substance in this shadow world, and how can one not expect the gravest misgivings when one talks about light and they can only picture darkness?

Best I stay silent and keep walking.

Truly, I am an outcast in this strange, ghostly land.

Tears Upon The Battlefield

A young friend sat alone on the grass in the central city park unnoticed by those who were too busy. Writing poetry that surpassed her age she was a defiant heart crying in the shadows of our so-called civilisation.

Struggling inwardly and bravely, her poetry whispered to me like a beautiful song that both kissed and saddened my heart.

Smiling as I approached, Madison dropped her pen and notepad in her bag and stood up to give me a warm hug. Taking her hand with a smile I guided her through those quieter and unpopulated streets and pathways. As we navigated our way through the city, we talked and laughed and the throb and blur of our surroundings went unnoticed.

Coming to a footbridge she skipped on ahead and ran up the stairs.

Sometimes we would come here to talk and reflect. A true reality check in a world gone mad and we were blessed in a simple friendship by its living flame as we struggled within the limitations of our earthly sojourn.

We walked out to the centre of the bridge, the city stood before us and its traffic moved beneath. Together, we stared out over the urban sprawl...

"Sometimes I get so scared," she broke the silence between us. "This civilisation has lost all sense, and the people go about their mundane lives in a way that no longer has any true meaning. Our society seems void of purpose, everything is confused and often wrong."

She looked up at me questioningly. "It seems so overwhelming."

As I stood beside her, I could feel her deep concern and troubles.

"When humanity denies truth they lose their alignment and connection to Life," I answered. "The wheel turns, a new cycle begins, all that we have invested in disappears, all that we have created turns around and bears down upon us.

"Should we seek to cling to the familiar and the comfortable now we find they are disappearing. The world as we know it is coming to its end."

Bitterly she whispered: "This world is insane. Every day our teachers, media and peers sell us lies as truth, conformity as individuality, prison as freedom.

"My heart tells me that humanity has lost its way because they call this life," she pointed out to the horizon, "when all it is, is walking death.

"My friends succumb to this fog having lost all sense of who they truly are. Their hearts are dying and their minds corrupted by the propaganda of a decaying world order that seeks to keep them confused, sickened and distracted."

I looked into her eyes and said:

"We shed our tears upon this battlefield as we watch the tide of death take many out to sea. Yes, today we are forced to face the collective projections of life that is going wrong. Those who can hear must arouse their hearts and hearken to Truth for if they do not wake up fast they shall drift into a collective nightmare.

"This is the cost of a society heedless to the truth of the times and a people who have strayed into apathy, materialism and blind indifference.

"A world that has fallen deep into self-absorption wherein everyone has become so confused, weak and powerless."

"What you say speaks to my heart but it is so hard," she answered. "Humanity has become so psychologically sick there is not enough true light to discharge this rising madness. The burden seems too great.

"I feel we have been abandoned by our elders and left to fend for ourselves in a world that has lost all hope and meaning. We are a targeted and easy prey for this ruthless, material civilisation that exploits its children to fatten itself.

"No one wants to listen; no one seems to care."

She looked away, down over the traffic.

I replied: "It takes a strong heart and mind to wade clear of this madness that threatens to claim us all. The cross of humanity is very heavy and this world seeks to deny its conscience by silencing the true servers of the race.

"In their denial they have burdened their children under the weight of the age."

I took her hand before continuing. "But remember, great are the forces of Love that lie beyond the periphery of human sight. Humanity's true guides are ever present — they shall always aid those whose hearts are sincere." I smiled softly.

She whispered: "But humanity is living heedless to what is transpiring.

"Deaf and inert do they live their lives. Their hearts so dull, their heads filled with so many trivial and dead things.

"They have become so lost that they know not they are."

Fire flashed behind her eyes. "This world shall not claim me!" she exclaimed defiantly.

I smiled at her bravery. "It is living intuitively and selflessly that is true rebellion in a world twisted in lies, selfishness and deceit. We must live from our true centre of being should we withstand this illusion as the world does roar.

"Collectively, we are now being forced to face the self-created demons of our past as this juggernaut of civilisation rises and what we have unleashed seeks to draw us into conflict and war.

"We must face this openly, honestly and bravely."

She looked out into the distance. "Within my heart there are visions not of this world. A remembrance of the Greater Life arouses from within. I have a call to inspire and awaken those who smother this sight by their own hands and foolishness."

I whispered: "Trust in the guidance of your heart and live your life selflessly, in such a way as to invoke that true Grace that seeks to help you.

"Let your writing be, as your soul guides you to serve the race.

"In a time of confusion and world deceit you have the true honesty to confront those self-deceptions within and around you. You arouse those sleeping hearts to their true divine nature. That is rare, and to live in such a way takes a selfless heart."

Together we looked out beyond the smog hazed horizon.

Her voice broke, "But sometimes I feel so alone…"

I put my arms around her and a soft vibration of divine Love rippled the ethers around us. It touched her heart and she swelled with grateful tears.

I smiled. "No, you are not alone and when your work here is finished the Kingdom awaits you."

So Does A Lie Meet Its End

You have erected great cities
Concrete, metal and bold
Tall buildings and structures
Which are but tombstones
Offset a smoking horizon,
A subconscious defiance
Upon the cusp of great change;
Children at play
In their own graveyard,
A people reflecting
Their hardened hearts
And rigid minds
Unwilling to let go
Unable to open
Trapped in a decaying thought
Which they will not repent.
It is but a civilisation
Breathing its last breath
Not unlike worms
Feeding upon a corpse

Your priests
And your prophets
Chant mantras of death
Beating upon a drum.

LIVING MOMENTS

Estranged
From the cosmic pulse,
Attuned
To the sickened heartbeat
Of fallen life
In which you are all but devils
Dancing in a ring
Of false light
Prostrating yourselves
Before a shadow,
A black and unholy creation
Which has turned upon you
And made you its slave.
Oh, hypocrites and fiends,
Betrayers of Life,
Servants
Of the defiled Word
Generation after generation
You have thrown your children
Upon an anvil
To beat in your master's will
Forging them to a program
Of a tortured and twisted mind
Burning in the fires of hell
A lineage of death
Begotten of the great beast
That eats its own children
And has usurped your hearts.

Planning, plotting
Scheming and deceiving
Is the antichrist
Working inside you,
A wayward intelligence
That would rationalise
Its own madness,
An arrogance
That would stamp its mark
In time
In defiance of change
But a great desperation
And effort of futility
In this dark ocean
Of impermanence,
And behind your eyes
Shine its darkened will
And your smiles
Are but a thin veneer
Of hypocrisy
That would veil
An amalgamation
Of lies and deceit,
Such is the terror of a lie
Afraid of being unmasked.

Take heed, oh humanity
To this living testimony

LIVING MOMENTS

Of the immovable race.
Silent witnesses
Standing amongst you
Of an event that you are in
But will not see,
A world at war
With its own soul
Defying its conscience
The great battle being played
Within the hearts of men.
Now as Judgement draws near
We ask you,
Must our cry be in vain?
For we see
That you shall cling
To a reality false,
To this illusion enforced
By its own denial,
An old and crumbling house
That you will not leave
Though its foundations are shaking
Upon a ledge
That can no longer support
That shall have you tumble
Into an abyss.

For though your world
And your dreams

Lay in waste
You have spurned
The offered hand
And revel like swine
In a dung heap,
And now we must watch
As your world
Crumbles around you
Knowing that you
Make your dying stand
Upon the very quicksand
That shall consume you.
And so does a lie
Meet its end.

A Waltz To Remember

On a night of a full moon, gentle spirits were beckoning me to a familiar rock on a small hill that sat overlooking lush fields of a nearby valley. It was upon this rock that I often found solace to sit and contemplate.

As I walked up the hill, the night sky glittered brilliantly.

The moon's silvery white light lit up a path before me, bathing the trees around me in its soft luminescence. The night was still and mystical.

Reaching the top of the hill, I noticed the glow of a small fire on the rock and a shadowed figure sitting silently, staring out into the night sky.

I approached quietly to see an elderly woman wrapped in a light shawl. Her black hair was streaked with silver that seemed to reflect the very starlight sparkling above us. I did not know her ethnicity but glancing at her, it seemed she might have come from any one of the tribes of Earth. There in the moonlight I silently mused, because it felt she might just be all of them.

Her deep black eyes looked out into space. She was unmoved by my approach.

I invited myself to sit next to her so that I could share the glorious view of the star filled firmament.

"Dear old mother," I said, "what brings you here this night?"

She turned and looked deeply into my eyes. There was an unfathomable depth in her stare. Though she wore the body of an elderly woman, I was in the aura of a powerful spirit.

I stared back at her wonderingly. I was trying to feel out who or what she was when a voice whispered on the breeze... the Great Grandmother.

A long moment passed. Her presence felt as ancient as the moon.

"I'm not that old," she said eventually. I knew she was reading my mind. She smiled playfully, and then gave me a flirtatious wink!

I smiled back bashfully. Her deep eyes sparkled as spiritedly as a young child's yet her poise commanded respect as her strong presence overshadowed her aged appearance.

I wondered what was to become of this strange auspicious night. Why had I been led here?

"My dear boy, my sweet child, take my hand," she said in answer to my thought.

She opened her weathered hand, which I softly took in mine.

There on the hilltop we both shut our eyes.

I was released into a vision of dreaming. I watched the skies turn quickly, rotating from night to day. I observed the Earth's seasons change in a visual collage of timelessness. I saw continents shift, forests grow and seas change in a flowing graphic of beauty that was played in my mind's eye.

I felt light and buoyant. The vision kept going as I watched in awe.

I saw the journey of humanity throughout the ages, witnessing the rise and fall of great civilisations and strange things to behold. I observed alien realities manipulating the human race and realised that humanity's long history was far different from what anyone of this modern age could perceive.

The Grandmother Spirit had been there through it all.

As I contemplated what I had just seen, the vision shifted.

I became a little girl walking through a field of flowers remembering the ethereal innocence of a young child as I ran, danced and played.

Upon a storyboard of a feminine life playing out before me, I quickly shifted in years. I became a young teenager staring out under the stars, yearning for love. I felt a young girl's beautiful dreams and high aspirations.

The vision kept going...

I was a young woman finding her first lover...then felt the tears of first heartbreak, the confusion and pain. I felt courage return and a new love come. I watched the struggles and dramas of an earthly life. Experiencing the birth of my first child, watching my children grow with love and seeing them leave with heartache. I witnessed my life change and my husband grow old in an incessant visual stream of joy and sadness, heartbreak and hope. I felt the cruel touch of time, the ageing of my body.

The tone of the vision shifted again. It became faster…

I felt the loss of loved ones, loneliness and despair. I saw young men recklessly run off to war…images of horror, violence and brutality. I felt the worry of mothers for their children, the yearning of wives hoping for their partners to return; the Earth being destroyed. The madness of the modern world swirled around me in a vortex of painful imagery of hopelessness and anguish. It kept going; the vision had become almost frantic.

I reeled and let go of the Great Grandmother's hand to stop the vision.

I felt the Grandmother's pain, there was a tear rolling down her cheek.

"I have known many ages…and none has been so strange as this one," she said.

With a look I questioned her.

I felt the shame.

She looked into my eyes and read my heart. Her face softened and she said in gentle recognition, "I see you and I are not so different."

She was gazing into my being, tracing the lines of incarnations and cosmic pre-Earth journeys.

I knew what she meant.

The rise and fall of the great civilisations of Earth are nothing but faint ripples upon the ocean of life. The lifetimes of men are but a bauble in space, and all will vanish into nothing but distant memories in the shadows of time.

And what would become of this wayward world?

LIVING MOMENTS

The glories of so-called modern man are but dust. The vain and the powerful are destined to become but forgotten ghosts. This world civilisation is a towering monument of its disgrace, and here at its end nothing of this age would be left standing. Thus already inscribed upon the ethers was the sad epitaph of this Yuga.

And those of the deep silence had waited patiently throughout it all, watching and calling to humanity to understand and change its ways.

I smiled with a sad knowing and we held each other's gaze in the quietness.

There I pondered for many moments on the strange and wonderful events of this enchanting night.

The breeze had stilled, and it was then that a thought came to my mind. I rose to my feet.

Inspired, I held out my hand, bowing in a time forgotten chivalry.

Now it was she who stared at me questioningly and wonderingly. I smiled.

Curious, she stood up, taking my hand.

As I brought her to my chest I shared a dreaming of joy, hope and nobility. She looked down at herself, she had become young again. Looking into her eyes I shared a vision of a man looking into the eyes of his first love and together we embraced as we swayed gently together under the stars. We dreamed the healing of the Earth and a new humanity born into an age of wonder, and there we danced through the ages…

After a long and beautiful interlude we gently let go and released.

"Thank you sweet child," she whispered affectionately.

She leant forward and softly kissed my forehead then turned back to stare out over the moonlit valley.

She smiled as she spoke. "Now comes the Great Shift of seasons, the one I have waited for all my long years." There was a sense of expectation and joy in her voice.

We shared the silence staring out to the stars. As the night wore on, sleep began to come over me and my eyes grew heavy. The last vision I had of the Grandmother Spirit was her glowing silver white and then everything faded into darkness.

§

I awoke as the first rays of the dawning sun broke through the skies. The fire had become whispers of smoke and she had gone.

Standing up to look over the beautiful sunlit valley, I felt strong and rejuvenated.

A whisper entered my mind and I heard her voice – 'Grandma has given you a bath!'

I knew I had received a beautiful healing.

I giggled to myself at such a strange and beautiful night.

It was one I would never forget...

Months later, I was walking through a busy urban street in a major city. Unnoticed by the people rushing about was an old woman struggling with some shopping bags, trying to navigate the great current of city madness that was all around her. She had tripped up and no one seemed to care.

I walked up to her and offered my hand. She looked up and behind her eyes I saw a familiar glitter.

"My sweet child," the old lady said and gave me a playful wink.

I helped her to her feet and took her bags.

Together we walked through the urban indifference, smiling.

Strange Times

These are strange times, chaotic and unsure.
Smiling faces are the mask of a desperate and hidden war.
Rumours abound of an unearthly conspiracy,
Laughed at by the people as foolish absurdity.
Where evidence of deep state atrocity
Is covered up in disbelieving animosity.
Everyone is scared to admit to the truth
While poisoning the next generation's youth.

Those in denial all sing the same song.
Going about their lives like nothing is wrong.
But don't be fooled by this conflict of silence,
It is one of great inner violence.
People afraid to face what they must face,
Thinking their conscience can be erased.
A collective mind of this insane rationalism
Wear the jackboots of a new global authoritarianism.

As those in high despotism
Seek to wield this growing fanaticism,
Sweeping us up into a fallen angel's spell,
Trying to pull us into their technocratic hell.
And while we observe this with great sadness
We shall not succumb to this growing madness.
Tempered and strong and with the eye of the soul,
We are breaking through all their mind control.

LIVING MOMENTS

You needn't be afraid of what you see,
We are being called, to be set free.
Between the old and the new,
The many and the few,
Opens a growing rift
As the veils now lift.
Through the darkness shines a new light,
Revealing that which was hidden into plain sight.
And people are seeing what they didn't before
As the minds of the guilty try to conjure their war.

What we witness is not the end of Earth
But a new beginning, a planetary birth.
What is happening is beyond their comprehension
As we walk into a new dimension.
Beyond the limits of what they deem possible
We find ourselves realising the unfathomable.
These "End Times" are but the beginning for some,
Who aren't afraid to come undone.

Ignore dark whisperers and what they say,
We are rising to greet the new day.
As the shadows of yesterday disappear,
We shall know there is nothing to fear.
At the end of all that is history
Marks the unveiling of a great mystery.
As we stand to meet in the new vibration,
That brings us to true consciousness liberation.

When The Lights Go Out...

It was night and the rain poured down heavily outside. Thunder shook the heavens as an electrical storm brought down the rage of the winds damaging the city's energy grid. The lights went out and we sat in darkness.

I lit a candle on a small table in the living room.

My friend Monique sat next to me in a reclining chair, she was greatly saddened by what was revealing itself in the world as we both pondered the powerful and often disturbing revelations of the times we lived in. Rumours were surfacing about the elite and ruling class of the world, with evidence emerging of horrors and acts of hidden depravity, of child trafficking, ritual sacrifice and cannibalism.

It was an auspicious moment to share insight into such things.

She looked at me in despair. "Is it true?"

I met her look in the flickering candle light.

"The wealthy and powerful over generations of miscreant rule, long ago lost themselves to involutionary magic and thus to madness. I can assure you that what you are hearing is only the smallest part."

She sat, thoughtful. "Is this why we are being attacked in our own homes and in every aspect of our lives through our televisions, radios and computers? It feels as though we are being hypnotised and programmed to accept their culture of death. The more I investigate it seems every facet of society has been infiltrated. People are so lost and confused, programmed into believing the lies and false narratives given them. Fear has overridden their sanity and often they turn on each other. I know we cannot trust anything that the media says anymore."

"Yes," I said, "it has all been infiltrated and much goes on behind closed doors. As this world awakens, the family of dark seek to keep humanity chained and powerless. Those of the shadows have merged with alien means, using all possibilities at their disposal to subvert and capture humanity dragging them into their advancing technocratic hell."

Thunder rumbled outside, shadows flickered on the wall from the dim candlelight that cast an eerie glow.

There was such sadness in her eyes. "Where did it all go so wrong?"

"There are entities," I began, "that exist in spheres that are sealed from human awareness, yet if we are not vigilant as a race, they can rise and consume us. When we venerate the material over our inner spirit and become too selfishly inclined, we can fall victim to beings that exist in realms beyond the threshold not meant for us. It is to these the elite make their sacrificial oblations."

Her voice broke in angrily. "We need to run them down and make them pay for their crimes!"

"Yes, these things are now to be brought to an end," I replied dispassionately.

"However, in this convoluted world the line between perpetrator and victim are not so easily drawn. I can assure you that many have sought in humanity's past to run down such evil, never seeming to catch it. Falling even deeper into their illusions, many of the so-called righteous became what they themselves had reviled. Before we lose ourselves to hatred and condemnation we must first see how we feed this very evil around us."

"What do you mean?" she asked with a confused look.

I met her look. "I call on you to look within and see the murderer, liar and thief inside yourself!"

She stared at me, shocked by my words.

I kept speaking.

"Look around, do you think yourself so innocent?

"We have sold our brothers and sisters of humanity to a slave culture in want for material luxury. We have turned our backs on the raping of the Earth. With the words that you speak and the decisions you make, what have you been in consent with?"

Seeing her confusion, I continued.

"This act of planetary transmutation must come from within. We must see how we ourselves participate in this matrix of death and take back our sense of deeper responsibility. It will be hard because these late generations have seen humanity revelling in great selfishness and denial.

"Know that before we can even see the true solution, we must first face our own shadows!"

Tears welled up in her eyes. "It is all so confusing."

She looked at me a little angry and rejecting "It seems you would make us vulnerable. In a time of madness you would have us give up our self-defence. You are scaring me."

I replied: "In truth, the deeper problems of this world are now way beyond human capacity to deal with. There are great divine energies and beings that have been drawn to Earth at this time of planetary change. We are called to align with the new energies entering the Earth – with them lie our healing and true protection. In holding this alignment the filth of the world is being brought to the surface to be cleared. We are being called to become conduits of such energy."

"How can one know what you say is true?" she asked.

"You seek a security for yourself that I cannot give," I replied. "In times of darkness you cannot rely on the outer senses; and do you think that in trying to cling to your illusions you are safer?

"Now it is time to face your fears."

I leaned toward the table and blew out the candle.

We sat in the silence letting her ponder deeply on what I had said. I felt confusion and resistance arise in her mind and felt her fear at what was being revealed.

My voice pierced the darkness. "If you look out, you will only succumb to darkness and confusion. How can you defend yourself when the enemy is seemingly everywhere?"

"You have a deeper light," I continued, "that can see through the illusions of this world but you must be willing to seek the truth and find your true centre. Know that when the lights go out, if you let go of fear, the real can awaken."

I could feel her intense struggle.

Thunder boomed, the rain poured harder. Trees thrashed in the wind. The world outside seemed like it was destroying itself.

My voice echoed, "We must overcome this evil not by looking outside of ourselves but by first looking within."

I could feel her turmoil; she wanted to run away but in the darkness there was nowhere to run and in the blackness of this night there was nothing to grasp for comfort. Alone and in the dark, she was forced to sit with her madness and fear. I felt her panic and despair because here there was no one to attack or to blame.

She broke out into a deep sobbing.

I remained silent and a long time passed. There, in the deep silence of the long dark moment, she eventually let go. Facing her self-delusion and madness, having seen the deeper truth, she gave up her fear.

Together in the pitch blackness we relaxed in the storm and breathed deeply, at one with the night. There Monique opened the eye of her deep intuition, piercing the shadows and darkness.

"I feel that we should not be hypnotised by the lies and illusions the family of dark have cast before us," she said. "All this technocratic sorcery is but a psychological trick…they have used us to build our own prison cells. It is we in our fear who have given them substance and power over us."

"Yes," I said, "that is why we are asked to let go of this world of illusions. Do you understand?"

"Yes." In a strong impersonal voice she spoke the words; "it is the world of the personality that is the illusion. We are called to take leave of this madness."

"What do you see?" I asked.

"I can see their time is done!" her voiced boomed.

Then lightning flashed and thunder cracked all around us.

Your Reign Now Ends

Oh wayward brother
Your hands are stained red
And you hide them
Behind your back.
Your legacy of generations
Flows as a river of blood,
And now at its end
Shall you drown
In your own filth.
Adorned in robes
Lined with stolen jewels
That sparkle lacklustre
As do the stars
In Lucifer's firmament
Do you bow your heads
Before a reverted cross,
Servants of death
Commanders of the hordes,
The very cancer
Consuming this planet.

You who know nothing
You who hear nothing
Except the sound
Of your own loud voices

LIVING MOMENTS

Whence do you think
Your salvation comes?
Clinging to images
Of saints and saviours
Long departed
You pray only to shadows.
Know your phantoms
Cannot save you
And from whence comes
Your authority?
Burnt offerings
And empty speeches
Only pollute the ethers
Expounding your corruption
Revealing your lack
Of true acquaintance
For your rites and ceremonies
Have been reduced
To a failing sorcery
Enslaving the weak
Through aeonic manipulation,
Imitators and adulterers
Know your father
Is a liar.

Now take heed
Oh poisoned priests
The destiny

Of the ages is nigh
And the sword of right
Shall be dipped
Into this pool of stagnancy
For no longer
Shall your rest
Be found in its arrogance
And you shall tremble
Before the thunder
That comes
And it is given us
To torture your hearts
With the word of Life
And trample your death
Under our feet
And you will revile
Making war with us
Yet we the children
Of Life
Shall laugh in your face
For do you think this world
Means anything to us?
Know you may slay the image
But not the Life
For it lies
Beyond your reach.

LIVING MOMENTS

And before the light
Of the living Christ
You shall see
The darkness and death
That is self
And you shall howl
And lament
Over the falsehood
And madness
You have wrought
For we shall overcome
And in dispersing desperation
We see that you shall
Cling to your idols
In shame and in dread
But all is in vain…
For "Our Father"
Is of the living
And heeds not
The dead

Your reign ends now.

WOW

My friend Kate came to visit the newly built apartments where I was briefly residing in a South-East Asian country. It was very hot and humid so we hurriedly removed her bags from the taxi and after saying goodbye to the driver, I took her into the air-conditioned complex where I was staying.

Taking out my security pass I slid it over a small sensor which opened the gate and we passed by the security guards in their windowed room who were monitoring the complex through their CCTV cameras and screens. They smiled and saluted as we walked past.

She looked at them a little reserved. We both come from the countryside of Australia and were not used to such formal protocols and security measures. We quickly walked into the apartment lobby where there were plush leather seats and couches that adorned the space with lighted fountains that glowed artificially opalescent. There were many large pot plants throughout the area and lining the walls.

She looked around and then looked at me. "Wow," was all she said.

Then walking towards one of the tropical pot plants she reached out and touched it but only to recoil. "It's fake," she said as she looked at me questioningly.

I laughed at her surprise. "They are all fake." I gestured at the entire room and she looked around the lobby frowning, reassessing what she first thought to be real plants.

"These modern apartment complexes boast cleaner and more sanitised living in Asia than what has been available over the last decades," I said. "These are the so-called new eco-housing developments that are springing up all around here and the rest of the country." She looked at me in disbelief.

"Come, let's get up to the apartment." I smiled.

We walked out of the lobby, passing many posters on the wall that showed people in recreation. 'This Is Living' was written in bold print on them, referring to the apartment complex we were in.

I took out my security key and swiped the glass security doors as we continued to walk to the elevators.

As we stepped into the elevators, I swiped my security key again over a small pad before typing the floor number we were in. As we ascended to our destined floor the elevator wished us a good day. We then walked down another hallway lined with barred metal doors to reach our apartment. Placing my finger on a biometric pad on the door it read my fingerprint, then it opened and we walked inside.

The apartment was very small but tidy. I had been renting it the last couple of weeks from a website I had found on the internet. In the centre of the main room was a large TV which, according to a small booklet beneath it delivered Wi-Fi, kára-oke and other sorts of conveniences and amusements. Besides that, the rooms were sparsely furnished, air-conditioned and fitted with various smart appliances and lighting.

I smiled at her, "Why don't you have a shower and get changed," as I pointed to her room. "And when you are done join me out on the balcony."

She smiled back glad at the offer, needing to refresh after her flight.

About half an hour later she walked out of her room refreshed. I was sitting on a chair on the small balcony lined with artificial grass and flowers as she came through the curtained glass doors to join me.

She looked out from the balcony. "Wow," was all she said.

We looked out over a large pool that resided in the centre of the apartment complex. Palm trees lined the pool and as the sun was going down there were many small fountains lit up around the complex that started to change colours. We could hear the crashing of waves and between the buildings see the ocean in the distance.

She looked at me with a frown and said, "I didn't know we were that close to the ocean?"

"We aren't," I replied. She looked at me a little weirded out.

"What you see is part of a projected illusion of water from a screen between those two buildings," I explained. "What you are hearing is from hidden speakers around the complex."

I laughed. "Welcome to what is called resort-style living. Its popping up all over these cities and each apartment complex has its own theme."

"Wow," she said again.

She raised an eyebrow and said, "At first glance it looks so real and impressive but it's all so artificial. These apartments are actually very small and wouldn't everyone be constantly bombarding each other with artificial frequencies from their phones and computers? How can they call this eco living?"

I laughed. "I have been asking myself the same thing since I arrived here a couple of weeks ago. At night I can hardly sleep, I am way too sensitive to all this EMF.

"Do you want to hear something really strange?"

She nodded.

"Would you believe that last night I saw a cloaked UFO come down over these very apartments and pulse certain frequencies through them while almost everyone was sleeping. I suggest they are using people's Wi-Fi and smart appliances to carry certain signals that alter our energetic bodies and dreaming patterns. They are seemingly doing this so they can collect our residual emotive energy as a sort of loosh for their own means and food."

"Wow," she said again a little more uncertain and questioning.

"You have always been a strange one!" she jested, however she knew of my extra-sensory abilities.

I replied: "What do you think my chances are of getting society to understand that we are being used and experimented upon by aliens and that these high and compact apartment buildings are really nothing but energy harvesting stations?"

She raised an eyebrow and said, "Good luck with that!"

Then I spoke in a more serious tone and pointed to the apartments around us. "All this so-called smart technology is very dangerous in the hands of our wayward leaders and governments. Can you feel where it is all heading?"

"Where are you going with this?" she looked at me.

"When you remove the palm trees, the colourful pool and the posters telling you 'this is living', what do you see?" I replied.

"What do you mean?" she asked a little more confused.

"I am getting you to see that with one flick of a switch what people are calling secure and high living can become instant imprisonment."

She looked around at the tall clustered apartments, the security guards, high wire fencing and the many CCTV cameras.

"Wow," she said again.

She looked at me and her face was very troubled as we pondered together on the balcony.

The Left-Hand Path

When the truth is hard,
It is easy to blanket oneself in illusion.
When we refuse to face our pain,
It is easy to keep distracted.
When we don't want self-responsibility,
It is easy to just keep on going.
Shadows are an easy place to hide.
Who cares that the smiles are false
Or the air is poison
Everyone knows, yet nobody admits.
There in the denial of Life,
It is very easy to blame others.

Yet as the light sears through the darkness
All will soon grieve and ask,
"How did we get here?"

But would I speak to you now
Of the Right Path to God,
You would just trample me to the ground
As you run in the other direction.
Too busy to care or to acknowledge
Because it is easier...

Through The Veil

As I sat on a park bench under the dim glow of a terrace street light, Asha walked over to me.

The deep and heavy problems of this wayward world often weighed heavily upon her heart. Often we would seek the sanctuary of each other's company in the night and under the stars.

Staring into the darkness we held each other's hand as we contemplated a tired and outworn humanity. A world, merciless and harsh. A people so lost and yet so arrogant. A society that was so loud yet so afraid.

Today, we could see a collective that had become imprisoned within its own self-created madness, running into the dark chasms of its own repetitive and bloodied past. Here were a people unheeding of the signs that flashed blatantly before them.

Her eyes glistened with tears as she softly let go of my hand.

"The people of this world are like caged animals that have forgotten that which lies beyond their bars," she cried softly. "I feel their pain and separateness, yet, should I reach out my hand in love they would only swipe at me in fear."

I looked at her. "I know why you cry, for I too shed the same tears. Humanity has lived heedless of truth and that which has been forewarned.

"Now they begin to tremble before that which they have created."

She whispered: "Great is the pressure upon their hearts and minds as the Divine Fire bears down. Unwilling to face their true predicament many are burying themselves deeper in their illusions. This is only creating great pressure and engendering greater fear. Deaf to true guidance, possession grips this world. Now it shall break into madness."

She looked up into my eyes. "Why do they fail to see the truth? That until all this egotism is conquered, the door of Life will remain shut. Until the prince of this world is brought to his knees, the transcendental shall remain hidden and inaccessible. Divine Love will not find its way into the hearts of men!"

"Yes," I smiled weakly. "Hiding in the darkness, humanity revels in its madness! As the world ego struggles against itself, despair and anxiety grow. This is the product of those who stand in fear of Life, ignorant of Truth. Pushing their denial into extremities, they will continue to spiral downwards into increasing fear and negativity. It is under cosmic impetus that all is being brought to the light and now there will be no place to hide as global processes accelerate and this degenerate civilisation is brought to its end. The Divine Fire will purify this world!"

"Yes", she answered, "driven back by the fire of Love the world ego faces its death. Hard are the realisations to be faced by those who can heed the truth of these times...as we must now struggle through the madness of this world."

She looked at me helplessly. "This dying world order struggles to maintain its rotten existence instead of submitting to Truth, humanity in its blindness would rather run to conflict and annihilation!"

I answered: "Yet by facing death itself humanity could release those qualities of heart and soul that they have buried under all their lies and deceit to understand that which is real.

"If those who could but hear and understand the real liberation in truly confronting such an event, they would realise it is time to face that which must be faced and to seek the essential. Then the false glitter of this fallen world will lose its attraction and the Truth within them could be revealed.

"Then many could understand that beyond the veil of death even within all this madness...Love is waiting!"

She took my hand. "We must not partake in the growing insanity but shall bear the harsh reality and affliction of this hour. Love does summon and we are ever led onwards."

"Yes", I replied, "do not fear, we are called in an hour seemingly bereft of light yet it is within this darkness that the Truth calls to those sparks that seek the greater communion. Today, only those pure of heart can heed and respond to such a call."

Looking out into the darkness she sighed: "How do we stand within such madness?"

Taking back her hand, together, we fell on our knees in supplication.

Looking upwards towards the heavens did we still our hearts and minds as the shadows of the world danced and played around us.

Surrendering within, in the darkness of the night did the veil of death dissolve as the Light Supernal descended upon us.

Thy will be done…we prayed in the deepest silence of our hearts.

My Love

Drink, my love
Let your soul have its fill
For the world is a desert and you
Have lost your way.

Rest, my love
You are safe within my arms
Your eyes tell me of your weariness
And I know you are tired of walking in circles.

Cry, my love
Let me weep with you
Let me lighten the burden of your heaviness
For your tears and my tears bleed from one heart.

Pray, my love
I will kneel beside you
Together we will ask the heavens to lessen
the sting of the whipping winds
And to send loving rain to cool the scorching
sands that blister your feet.

Strength, my love
Be not thwarted by the fire of the sun,
It tempers the soul
And there are still many more dunes to cross.

LIVING MOMENTS

Faith, my love
It will lighten your footsteps in the sinking sand
And pick you up when you stumble,
For it is best not to fall in exhaustion when
hungry vultures circle.

Courage, my love
Is to follow the heart and take up your calling
Let it take you beyond this merciless place,
Paradise is waiting.

Do not give up, my love
Here we are but footsteps in shifting sands
For this life is not unlike a dream
And awake you will when you realise
That now is the beginning and end of
Every journey.

And your purpose?
It is Love, my love
And when you come home from your long parting
You will never be separate again.

Love In A Living Moment

Dust particles danced in the light of the sunlit window. My friend smiled as I walked into the room.

That week there had been a steady precipitation of higher energies and currents which had brought a subtle change of direction to an awakening experience we had been unfolding into.

It was a soft call of the soul that had called us together.

Life energies gently surged through my being and her beautiful eyes sparkled with a receptive shine. There was no need to speak because everything was seen in the living moment.

We drew close as she looked into my eyes with such purity of being that my heart opened and rejoiced as I met her beautiful gaze.

Gently touching her face, subtle electric currents flickered between us in a soft transmission of love. Safe and relaxed in each other's presence, we had nothing to hide from one another.

My spirit was stirred tenderly as she opened her being to me as a soft song of love played upon the ethers. Playfully we smiled to each other as we began to undress.

With a glance she beckoned me to the other room and I followed. I picked up a small candle and matches from the sunlit window sill as we went.

We then sat cross-legged on the floor, naked and unabashed before each other.

A light and beautiful energy washed through the room as we looked into each other's eyes. I lit the small candle and placed it next to us as we shut our eyes to give thanks to the Divine Mother. Her gentle and pervasive presence blessed the space. With soft ethereal whispers of light, we could feel protective gentle spirits dance into the room.

The ritual was sweet and touching yet it was our openness to Life that evoked the living spirit to play with us.

As we came back to meet each other's gaze, I gently brought her on top of me as she wrapped her legs around my body. I did not enter inside her. There were no expectations or attachments, just the beating of our hearts and the offering of ourselves to God.

Together we embraced with a delicate kiss.

Slowly, rhythmically, we harmonised our breathing, inhaling and exhaling as we let go of our surroundings. Unfolding yet simultaneously merging, we gently collapsed into a still point that lifted us both into resonance with the cosmic breath.

Our breathing gradually went deeper as we gently clasped each other's bodies though almost not conscious of doing so. Together, we slowly looked up in unison, releasing into a realm beyond time and space, losing the relativity of our body consciousness.

Allowing the breathing to rise in a crescendo, lifting our energies higher through our bodies, we let them collapse in unison. As one our energy fields opened in delight, unfolding as a cosmic flower.

Beautiful living light gently radiated from above. We raised our hearts to meet this sensuous space as the energy flowed down, fluid and delightful.

Our bodies began to pulsate, her legs wrapped tighter around my torso and she rubbed firmly against my body. Our subtle bodies pulsed as one, the energies of Life swirled around us in a vortex of colour and I felt a glow of energy lift from my base washing upward through us to meet the downward flowing energies pouring through our crown in a splashing of soothing ecstasy.

My mind's eye opened as we were transported into a cosmic rapture. We started to dissolve in a suspension of time as we were lifted high into the exquisite love of the Cosmic Mother – flowing, glowing and spinning in a thrilling dance of unspeakable bliss. Divine spirits of Life crowned us in a euphoric dream as light pulsed through us in a joyous wave.

I felt the throbbing of my physical body somewhere far below. Then in a pleasing orgasmic surge of energy which released through my heart, I felt the powerful rush of liquid light through me…

It released.

In a timeless peak we dissipated into nothing and everything.

As we drifted down back into our bodies, we exhaled deeply as we softly collapsed into each other physically. Sweat glistened over our skin in the soft candle light. Then slowly as we met each other's eyes in such joyous acknowledgement, we expelled our breath which released us into a deep relaxation. We fell backwards gently on to the floor, her legs still wrapped around me as her naked arched body found the soft rug.

Then, deeply inhaling and exhaling we let go and released the experience as we lay there in silence.

There, a long, sweet and euphoric moment passed, we were regenerated and thrilled. Smiling in elation and wonder as the divine energies very slowly and tenderly dissipated.

§

Hours later, I sat bare-chested on the balcony taking in the sweet smelling rose that was in my hand. My friend was still naked and looking out over the world. The warm rays of the sun illuminated her body.

She spoke as she pondered: "It makes you wonder what people are doing, they have forgotten so much!" She looked at me with a loving smile watching me smell the rose.

"The true tantra is the dance with Life. It is you communing with that rose, it is me dancing with the rays of Father Sun, it is us opening to God. What people are forgetting is that every moment is a living moment..." she spun around in a pirouette to face me.

I looked at her fondly. She was radiant.

"In this world people think it is another that gives them happiness and so they take it from each other. They have forgotten the blessing of pure Life that would dance in their hearts if only they would stop clinging so hard to that which is confusing them. True sex has always been a divine communion."

"It's so crazy isn't it," she replied. "All this debased love only leads to pain and so much misunderstanding. How did our world get so twisted? I feel like shouting to everyone, just wake up…what are you doing?"

I laughed. "They would look at us as if we were the idiots. Perhaps they are not ready?"

She looked at me with a beautiful smile.

"Well, they are the idiots because they don't know what they are missing!"

She jumped into my arms and we broke into laughter.

Facing Beauty

I sit facing beauty.
She dances for me in grace and sings to me
with such gentleness that she sings in silence.

She wears a dress of suffering but reveals her
radiance as I glimpse flashes of her nakedness.

In her eyes are the suns and in her smile the
promise of Love eternal, all which she hides
under a veil of death.

But I have unmasked her.
I met her with an open heart and she does
not shy from my stare, for my eyes seek not
to covet something of her.

In such freedom she is a vision of purity that
throws bashfulness to the wind.

In her innocence she reveals all to me
And with her openness I am closed to all else.
And with our separateness, forever we are wed.
In my longing I am fulfilled.

Dance for me forever my maiden.

A Gift From The Stars

On a night of planetary alignment, four of us sat on the balcony of our remote country home.

The starry aurora of the Milky Way glistened spectacularly as we marvelled at the sparkling night sky. Losing ourselves to inward contemplation, we became absorbed into the profound silence pervading the darkness. A zero point of consciousness to which we let go in a deep exhalation. It was here and nowhere, we felt a soft approaching energy that started to enfold and pulsate through us.

For a moment my friend Emerald glanced at me curiously. She then smiled almost expectantly as she shut her eyes to breathe deeply.

From above, in a gentle precipitation of loving energy, a spaceship of indescribable luminosity, flashing and pulsating colours descended from the night sky to hover above us.

As we relaxed into the experience, our group consciousness was lifted into a higher frequency and field of soft electrical blue energy. We felt the constraints of our body-bound reality dissolve. Time and space melted into non-existence.

'You are safe…' The words were whispered into our minds.

'You are safe…' Again the words repeated.

Within my deeper being I felt a familiarity with the energies. I could sense true benevolence. A surge of love breathed through the four of us. Our physical eyes closed as we let go to the experience, yet all the while we were keenly aware of each other's presence within a psychic field of resonant unity.

The voice whispered continued assurance. In my mind's eye materialised a celestial being floating before me. A knowing from somewhere deep came to my consciousness; this being was known as Arcturian…

Though the remoteness of this race seemed far removed from Earth's reality and experience, through the mind the being and myself began to communicate via an array of words, glyphs and imagery. There was happiness as I was relayed that there had been an important victory in the greater cosmos, yet I also sensed a little sadness in that it might mean some trouble for Earth. Through the exchange I could feel my friends around me in various communions and healing, their hearts pulsating in love for the beneficial energies they were receiving.

Then another surge of love frequency pulsed through my being as I was lifted from my body to their spaceship. The exchanges and downloads became quicker as I was lifted in vibration, feeling plasmic energy wash through me. There was no fear through the entire process – if anything a deep sense of expectation, even longing.

I was aware my friends were still below going through a beautiful process as I raptured into bliss, unable to relate to the conscious mind. Messages were now rapidly encoding my being. What I knew was happening was a healing and reconnection with the thread of universal DNA.

In a sweet void of timelessness, awash in a frequency of bliss I stayed raptured. There is only a blurred remembrance of this experience yet I was deeply and inherently coherent throughout this beautiful process of inwardly familiar cosmic re-orientation. Though time was not experienced in a mundane sense, in earth relativity, it went for hours.

Drifting downwards as lightly as a feather, I was gently reinstated back into time and space. The delicate resurgence of my awareness that I was back in my body had me slowly opening my eyes to see my friends smiling up at the stars with grateful tears in their eyes. Their consciousness had also landed back into their bodies.

My friend Billie looked at me smiling; her heart seemed aglow and pulsing.

The celestial presence began to softly withdraw as the spaceship above us began pulsating. It was about to depart. As we watched, the sky opened above us as we momentarily glimpsed through a wormhole into which the ship was leaving. Beyond this window, there was lightning and flashes of plasmic energy that ominously crackled and rumbled as we glimpsed a tremendous cosmic battle being furiously fought in other dimensions. With a flash the ship left and the vortex dissipated.

Silence fell upon us and we hesitantly looked at each other, in awe and briefly stunned at what we had just seen. It had been a powerful and breathtaking vision.

We then felt a brief return of soft luminescence within our hearts and slowly a deep sense of wellbeing came over us. We laughed and smiled to each other.

We continued for a time staring out into the vastness of the night sky.

Thank you, we whispered to the cosmos, in deep gratitude for the gifts we had received from the stars.

The Dawn Lovers

One night, at a village feast held in honour of his return, Seth the poet left silently into the dark night, leaving the loudness and drunken festivity behind him.

Watching him quietly disappear, his beloved childhood friend Alexandra followed him into the garden. She found him alone and sitting under the luminous moon. Sitting down beside him she took his hand. "Why do you sit out here alone?"

He looked into her eyes and smiled.

"I sit by myself but never am I alone. Tonight I share the darkness with a bird whose cries echo throughout the valley and whose call beckons me to open my wings and fly with him. I sit by myself because who would sit with me and enjoy simple pleasures?

"Not they," he continued as he pointed to the drunken and loud figures raising mugs behind them.

"You judge them harshly," she frowned. "They are your friends and they celebrate your return."

His face grew hard. "They celebrate themselves for themselves; I am but an excuse for their own debasement."

Then his face softened as he explained. "They know not Love, only its pollution and those who don't know Love cannot know Life. Those who don't know Life cannot find Love, so they are friends to no one.

"They would rather sing their drunken songs of ignorance than listen to the truth. They would rather glut their senses in the presence of themselves than break simple bread with a stranger.

"They would rather pass out on wine than battle sleep to watch the sun rise. They would always rather something for themselves."

Alexandra sighed. "What you say may well be true but that is no reason for this self-imposed exile. There is no sense in your solitude. Join us back at the table."

Then Seth squeezed her hand. "Should you talk to me in reason then I will not answer because you cannot hear. Let us leave sense and its absurdities with the drunkards inside for they will tell you that they have it and that I am mad. Here under the moonlight I sit at a table of beauty, in there I sit with emptiness."

He looked out into the night and whispered: "You say it is I who sit in solitude but I say take a look behind you. You will see who has cut off their connection to Love and you will realise it is not I who is in exile and it is not I who am mad. It is they. They who mask their tears under a veil of drunkenness."

Then she looked back behind her...

That night two childhood lovers wrapped in each other's arms battled sleep to watch the sunrise.

Unutterable Love

As these weary eyes
Look over this darkened world
The wails of existence
Assail these ears.
Separate, isolated, confused
Must one traverse this veil of tears.
Humanity how you struggle
To shield the Truth from sight
Keeping each other cursed
In this never ending night.
Beloved Father,
Help me to let go
Of this sufferance of life,
I know this world is but a hell
Of confusion, pain and strife.
We are lost in this realm
Of unquenchable fire
Chained to these planes
By burning desire.
Do we sustain our own cause
At the cost of all
Every day in this prison
To re-enact the great fall.
Oh, Aurora of Love
Shine through the window of this soul

LIVING MOMENTS

Take me in thy caring hand
Unmake me so I can be made whole.
Claim me, loving Father,
Anoint me with your fiery Kiss
I'm unable to deny you
Not wanting to resist.
Oh, how this heart yearns
For such glimpses of light
And touches of grace
Boundless, transcendent, supernal
Before time, beyond space.

Unutterable Love
Christ calling me
Dissolve me in your radiance
To die to thee.

On A Starry Night

I sat on a chair looking out over the paddocks where I lived. The sun was setting and I pondered over the many strange and unexpected events that had happened to me in recent years.

My life had been turned upside down, having walked through an exploding public minefield of insinuations, blind accusations and deception from those who should have known better – people trying to make names for themselves with no care about the damage they were doing and totally oblivious to the deeper events that were happening around them.

I sighed.

Those who are unwilling to face their inner pain will often attack those who don't affirm their personal constructs of reality. Over the years I had come to know the madness of the world very well.

I watched the Sun disappear behind the darkening pastures.

It had felt good to walk away once again from the clambering and chaos of human egos. It had been time to leave those who could not hear the new call of Love that was being gently sounded beyond their personal horizons.

Darkness gently fell upon the land before me. I sat watching the spritely twinkle of the first stars that appeared in the night sky. As I stared out into space the firmament quickly burst forth with its bright adornment of sparkling diamonds. It was magic.

There, under the soft luminescence of the Milky Way, I wondered what the coming days would bring.

With this thought, I saw two stars detach from the night just above the darkened skyline. Shining magnificently, these two silent UFOs shot forward from the distance speeding directly towards me. I stood up out of my chair as they stopped very close, just above the veranda and I then watched them make a sudden shift of direction as they hurled themselves upwards into the sky.

I laughed as a beautiful energy gently surged through my being. Striving upward in an arc of beautiful streaming light they played and danced with each other in a double helix configuration.

My heart felt as if it was rising with them and I felt the worries and cares of this maddening world fall away from me.

Then in a bright flash, they disappeared.

I kept staring out into the vastness of space.

And I smiled.

In the presence of the Cosmos, how can one not be sweetly humbled by one's own insignificance?

Running Back Up The Mountain

The golden rays of the Great Central Suns permeated all of God's creation.

Within the temple of Love and sitting by the side of his smiling master, Anura (whose name means regal heart) held alignment with the Source of All. Absorbed in infinite wonder, his golden robe of light shimmered fantastically as together they meditated on top of the Holy Mountain.

Here, Life's blessings were dispensed throughout the worlds.

One day as they were immersed in the great effulgence of cosmos, a strange murmuring arose from the valley below and upon hearing it Anura became distracted. As he attuned to these odd and discordant sounds he heard the cries and pains of many suffering beings and was disturbed as he pondered upon the chaos far below.

His master, sensing his disciple's distraction asked, "What ails you my son?"

Anura answered: "Master, this moment I find it hard to hold my alignment. As the cries of those in the valley meet my ears, it disturbs my being to know there is such suffering in those people upon the Earth."

"Oh them!" his master chuckled.

"What do you mean?" asked Anura.

His master looked at him and replied, "They are all suffering from a little lunacy."

His teacher then went cross-eyed and swirled a finger around his ear!

But his disciple did not understand this well intentioned candour and just frowned all the harder. Sometimes he did not understand his master's sense of humour.

His radiant master looked at him fondly and spoke.

"Here upon the mountain, we bring Life to all of God's creation. If we neglect our duty then other worlds might suffer. Should those of the Earth seek their way out of the valley then nothing can truly stop them. They need only brave the mountain and thus we wait here to receive them."

"But master, no one comes!" Anura replied very seriously.

"It seems their cries are growing more desperate and I think it better if I went down to assist them. I will teach the way up the mountain to God. Nothing can deter me!"

The master looked into the eyes of his serious and grave disciple and he knew that look.

"I see you have made a choice and I know that nothing I can say will dissuade thee."

His teacher then stood up and walked over to a dimensional doorway on their left labelled 'The Shadowlands' and said: "The ways of this world are treacherous and dark, if the people see your radiance they will kill you. You will need to leave your golden robe here my son and put on worldly garb. Here in the holy temple I shall keep your golden robe and watch over thee."

Excited at the thought of helping humanity, Anura stripped off and put on a worldly robe. It had once been his master's robe long ago and had been saved for such an occasion. It was dull, colourless and very heavy but he would not let that deter him.

"God bless!" his master said as he opened the door.

Barely acknowledging his master, Anura did not see the tearful glint in his teacher's deep and knowing eyes, and with great enthusiasm and excitement he disappeared through the doorway to descend the mountain.

As he ran down the steep ravine he was so enthralled by his mission he hardly noticed the skies darkening with each step he took.

He pressed on down the mountain.

As Anura drew closer to the valley the air had become heavier and more polluted. The ethers felt lifeless and dense, and in a short while he realised he could no longer see the Sun. He hesitated for a moment as the strange sensation of fear pulsed through him but then he pressed on because he would not let that deter him.

Then as Anura entered the Earth, strange sounds hurt his sensitive ears and there was an awful smell.

LIVING MOMENTS

As he looked around he beheld many strange things.

Grey concrete monoliths towered over him through a polluted haze. Automobiles roared and beeped, unnatural lights flashed about him.

He paused to catch his breath. He felt queasy because the Moon above him made him feel quite sick and disoriented.

Everywhere it was very busy and noisy but what was even stranger was Earth's humanity!

No one noticed him or each other. People would just walk by in a strange hypnotic trance. Their smiles had no joy; their movements were discordant with Life. Their eyes seemed vacant and they looked very sick yet they kept going about their business as if nothing was wrong.

Yes...Anura thought. Things were very strange down here!

He became confused and a little fearful because he did not know what to do.

Yet the fire of enthusiasm burned in his heart and he would have nothing deter him!

So he decided to stay for a while, trying to learn their language in the hope of communicating with the people.

He went to their schools of education and philosophy, watched their strange televisions and even frequented their very popular cafes. Yet over time, all this only confused him more because though they chattered a lot, they didn't seem to know what they were chattering about.

Their words were all nonsensical.

He felt a little sad and frustrated. So in an attempt to connect with Earth's humanity, he thought to imitate them for a while and began walking around in circles, smiling to them as if nothing was wrong.

In a short time the Moon overhead began to completely disorient him. The heavy and polluted atmosphere began to make him tired and before long he fell asleep. In a strange state of dreaming he wandered around aimlessly with them.

Lost in this dreaming world, everyone was anxious and confused. The people did not realise they were asleep and they often argued with each other.

No one seemed to notice the strange black shadows that whispered incessantly into everyone's ear.

What was very strange was that everyone liked to wear heavy chains. In this dismal place the bigger the chains one had, the greater the social status. Some people wore chains so large and heavy they could not move.

It was very surreal because everyone struggled so intensely under their burdens yet no one wanted to get rid of them. This was because in this dream world, great chains were high-class fashion and everyone who wore them thought themselves a king!

Everyone was quite crazy.

People wailed and howled, others cried or laughed manically as they worked so hard to get nowhere. Confusion pervaded everything and nothing made any sense. Everything was upside down and inside out.

It was complete lunacy!

Anura started to be overwhelmed with fear.

Then suddenly, something fell from above and landed upon Anura's head, snapping him awake. He rubbed his sore head as he picked up a small stone. It was polished and its surfaces were reflective as a mirror. When he looked into it, catching a glint of light through the dark clouds above, he saw the smiling face of his beloved master and some words flashed through his mind...WAKE UP!

He looked around and wondered how long he had been asleep.

It seemed like lifetimes.

He remembered his divine mission – now nothing could deter him!

"Wake up!" he called to the people that walked about him.

But only a few of the people stirred and most of them just grumbled. They continued to go about their selfish business, bumping into each other, chattering incessantly and poisoning the Earth. They were all lost to their darkened dreaming.

Inspired, he thought to show them a better way.

So while they laboriously worked on meaningless things, he danced and sang before them.

They tried to ignore him.

As they bumped into and hurt each other, he would pick them up and heal them.

Yet they resented him.

He spoke to them about a Love that knows no bounds.

They grew suspicious.

Because he would not let them sleep, they grew angry.

Restless and disturbed in their slumber they began to circle Anura. Snarling, gossiping and threatening, he could hear the shadows in their dream world, whispering.

When Anura said he knew God, raising the mirror his master had given him to catch a small glint of light from the Great Divine Sun, they fell back, dazzled and confused. They called him evil; taking up their pitchforks and burning torches they attacked. Coming at him with a collective roar, they grabbed at his clothes and tore them off but Anura was light and swift of foot and jumped over them.

Naked, he took flight out of the valley. Like a comet, he tore up the side of the mountain as fast as his legs could carry him and nothing could deter him!

Nude and a little scared but with a sigh of relief he burst through the door into the master's temple. Panting and exhausted he looked up to see his master standing there with an expectant smile, holding his golden robes for him. Anura put them back on.

"What did you learn on Earth?" asked his master as together they sat down for a new planetary alignment.

Anura spoke thoughtfully: "One can offer the keys of Life but they will not free those who love their chains."

His master smiled. "Anything else?"

Anura added, "Yeah! Before we can teach them about God…those guys will first need to learn a better sense of humour!"

(Anura went cross-eyed and swirled his finger.)

They gazed at each other fondly and chuckled intensely.

It was good to be home.

Refugees Of Love

We sat silently around a campfire. My friend Jahve gently strummed his guitar in a sweet melody that seemed to evoke Life and dance in our hearts.

The spirit of the small mountains where we were staying was kind and feminine. She visited us with a whisper in our minds, pleased to know we could receive her and that we respected the sacred area. It was beautiful to feel welcome as we sat around the fire in a meditation with her.

My friend Emerald gently swayed to the soft music. Her deep eyes glinting, reflecting the light of the stars.

"The *new* is singing to us," she said as her beautiful smile shone with the radiance of the warm fire before us.

I looked into the night sky. I knew what she meant. The times were changing rapidly.

Those of us awakening to the new reality were contemplating the greater cosmic drama that was unfolding before us. Lives had been changed forever…

The fire crackled. The scent of the trees and flowers permeated the surrounds with a unique Australian aroma.

Pondering the events of the past months, she spoke. "If I would speak of what has transpired over these last months, I don't think anyone I know would believe me."

Our friend Billie laughed softly. "I don't think anyone could understand you," she said "The timelines are cleaving and the old world is failing. Those who cannot hear…it's best to leave them be."

I smiled, knowing the thoughts of my friends, their realisation of greater Life and their remembrance of their place amongst the stars. The *new reality* was already present. Here were the new seed of Earth and before my eyes they were already flowering.

Emerald continued: "The life that I once lived has become a fading dream. Its sickness apparent…the mindlessness of a civilisation so wrapped up in itself. It was never meant to be."

We all contemplated the fading dream of the dystopic reality we were leaving. The spirit of new Life was pervading our hearts; we were upon the shore of the New World.

"I don't think I could ever go back," Emerald mused.

We all pondered what she said silently for a while.

After a deep pause Billie asked, "Would you really want to?"

"Naaaaah…" Emerald exclaimed loudly, as we all started laughing.

A shooting star lit up the night sky above us.

We just smiled at each other as the heat of the fire radiated upon our bodies within our warm circle of love.

What Manner Of Love Is This?

You asked what manner of love is this?
That has estranged us from this world,
Where the laughter of human voices
Are but wails of pain and torment,
Where loneliness is one's closest friend.
We walk the path
And we struggle as the mud of the world
Clings to our feet,
Yet the call of Christ harkens our pace
And mostly we are blind
For the way is not seen with our eyes
But felt within our hearts,
And the dark ones laugh and whisper to us
"Fools, turn back, you shall become as dust".
But dust we know we already are
And turn back we shall not
For the thread of true Life we hold.
Unto its guidance we surrender
And naught can dampen our hearts' resolve
For this world means nothing to us.
And for this Love we walk the razor's edge
Towards new life that beckons us,
And upon this way we shall perish

Yet arise in glory and flame,
And when this earthly task is done
We shall disappear into the great silence of the dark
The Light of which man knows not,
The eternal spirit from whence we came.

www.ingramcontent.com/pod-product-compliance
Lightning Source LLC
Chambersburg PA
CBHW050438010526
44118CB00013B/1590